Unique – being the only one of its kind; unlike anything else.

Author: Jennifer Campbell

Illustrator: Pardeep Mehra

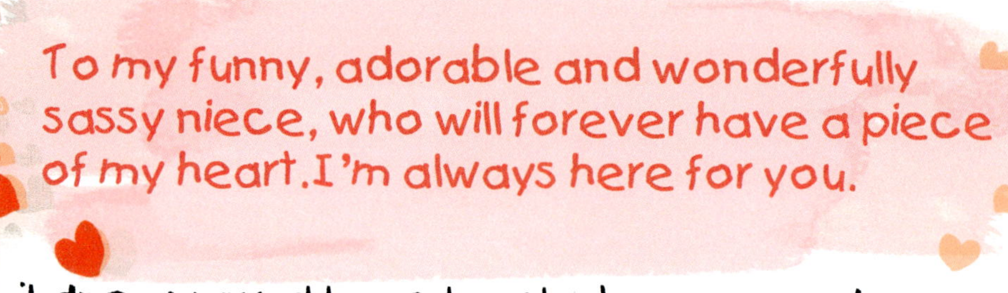
To my funny, adorable and wonderfully sassy niece, who will forever have a piece of my heart. I'm always here for you.

To the children: you all are lovely humans and a very important part of this world...question, ask, learn and grow.
Never be afraid to shine or try. Even if it seems scary.

To the grown ups: we all have struggles through life. Be loving and kind to each other, as well as yourselves.

Strive to be the best YOU that you can be because to be true to you, is the best form of love for all.

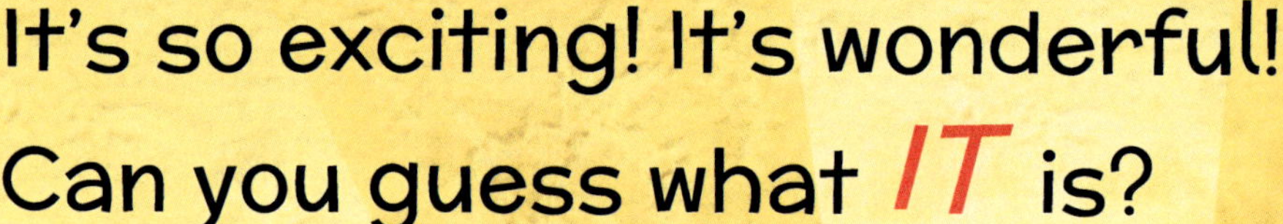

It's so exciting! It's wonderful!
Can you guess what *IT* is?

It's something so amazing...and so wonderful! And it's something about you - yes, YOU!

It's very, very important. It's something *YOU* need to know!

Are you ready to find out?

Here goes... You are *UNIQUE!* Yes, *YOU!* That's it! Do you know how unique *YOU* are?

From the moment you were born,
you were meant to be *YOU!*

You were born with many wonderful qualities that *YOU* are meant to share with the world!

Wouldn't life be dull if we were all the *SAME?*
Wouldn't it be boring?

Sometimes you may feel *SAD*, and you may wish you could be like someone else. It may not always be easy...to feel like other children are better than you.

But, guess what? It's okay to feel sad, as long as you remember that YOU are worthy and loved for who YOU are!

When you feel *SAD* and are thinking about being someone else, turn that frown upside down and be *YOURSELF*.

Be *extraordinary*. That means *awesome* and *amazing*. And that's what you already *are!*

If someone isn't nice to you, guess what?
It may not be because you are different.
They may feel sad because THEY
want to be like YOU.

It's so important to be KIND to others. We don't always know what kind of problem someone else might have. They may be very sad inside and just need to be treated kindly. Even a SMILE will help...

...and it's so important to know that we each learn, grow and play differently. Each and every person is a *blessing* to this world!

GOT
INSULIN

T21

Life is much better **because** we are different. We each have different personalities, abilities and skills. That way we can all **HELP** each other.

Each of us - with our own *uniqueness* - can work together to make the world a happier place.

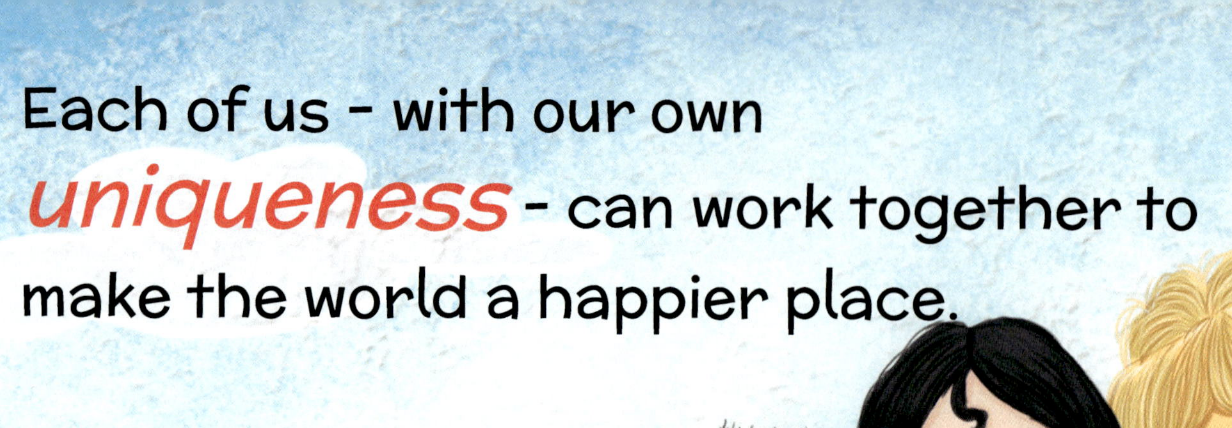

Your friends, and all the people around you, were born to be themselves - just like *YOU*.

Everything about you makes you...well... *YOU!*

From the thoughts in your head...
to the tips of your toes...

You were created to do great things. You are precious. *YOU* are one of a kind.

No one is *YOU*, and that is your *SUPER POWER*.

So...sing your own song...and dance to a tune that is all your own!

Be your own kind of you!

What do *YOU* think is unique and special about *YOU*?

My name is ____

Here is a picture/drawing of me.

I am unique because...________________________________

____

____

____

____

____

____

____

Eiram Media & Publishing
www.eirammediapublishing.com
For more information contact info@eirammediapublishing.com

Publisher's Cataloging-in-Publication Data
Provided by Adrienne Bashista

Names: Campbell, Jennifer, 1982-, author. | Mehra, Pardeep, illustrator.
Title: Unique starts with YOU! / by Jennifer Campbell ; illustrated by Pardeep Mehra.
Description: Raleigh, NC: Eiram Media & Publishing, LLC, 2019.
Identifiers: LCCN 2019911394 | ISBN 978-0-578-55741-0 (pbk.) | 978-1-7334087-0-7 (ebook)
Subjects: LCSH Self-perception--Juvenile literature. | Self-esteem--Juvenile literature. | Individuality. | Cultural pluralism--Juvenile literature. | Toleration--Juvenile literature. | Disability awareness--Juvenile literature. | CYAC Self-perception. | Self-esteem. | Cultural pluralism. | Toleration. | Disability awareness. | BISAC JUVENILE NONFICTION / Social Topics / Emotions & Feelings | JUVENILE NONFICTION / Social Topics / Self-Esteem & Self-Reliance | JUVENILE NONFICTION / Inspirational & Personal Growth | JUVENILE NONFICTION / Disabilities & Special Needs | JUVENILE NONFICTION / Diversity & Multicultural
Classification: LCC BF697 .C36 2019 | DDC 155.2--dc23

Made in the USA
San Bernardino, CA
26 November 2019